SOUNDING BOARDS

Oral Testimony
and the
Local Historian

Also available in the Local History Record Series

Diaries of Henry Hill of Slackfields Farm, 1872-1896
Edited by J. Heath

Life at Laxton 1800-1903: The Childhood Memories of Edith Hickson
Edited by B.A. Wood, C. Watkins, and C.A. Wood

Religion in Victorian Nottinghamshire: The Religious Census of 1851 (two volumes)
Edited by Michael Watts

Memoirs of a Loughborough Man: A.E. Shepherd 1872-1962
Edited by Joy Cross and Margaret Staple

The Local Historian's Glossary and Vade Mecum
Second Edition
Compiled by Joy Bristow

Also by David Marcombe

English Small Town Life: Retford 1520-1642
Studies in Local and Regional History, Volume 4

SOUNDING BOARDS

Oral Testimony
and the
Local Historian

David Marcombe

Department of Adult Education
University of Nottingham
1995

Centre for Local History Record Series no. 10

First published in 1995 by
The Department of Adult Education
Education Building
University Park
Nottingham NG7 2RD

ISBN 1 85041 075 5

Printed by Alden Press Limited, Oxford, England

CONTENTS

LIST OF ILLUSTRATIONS

The front cover shows a detail from Thomas Bewick's engraving of the old story-teller and the young listener from Joseph Ritson's *Robin Hood*, published c. 1795.

PREFACE

This booklet was written in an attempt to encourage more individuals and groups to involve themselves in the collection of oral testimony. Despite the involvement of 'academics' in this branch of study for many years now, too few non-professionals have taken up the challenge, partly, perhaps, because of a fear of the technicalities which might be involved. The following pages aim to illustrate that 'oral history' is a discipline in its own right but that it is also well within the reach and competence of the amateur researcher if certain simple guidelines are followed. The text is directed unashamedly at the beginner in the hope that increased awareness and knowledge will produce benefits for generations to come.

The text rests heavily on experience gained during the Nottinghamshire Oral History project which was operational between 1982 and 1984. This project was based at the University of Nottingham and was jointly directed by the University and the Nottinghamshire County Library Service. I would like to offer special thanks to my colleagues and research staff on that project, especially Robert Howard, Laurance Craike, Sheila Cooke, Derek Cox and our project supervisor, Dr Billy Patton. Our methodologies were worked out with much thought, experimentation and comradely co-operation, and hopefully they will be of use to others. As local historians we live in rapidly changing times when the recovery of oral data is perhaps more important than ever before.

David Marcombe
Centre for Local History
University of Nottingham

Chapter 1

THE ORIGINS OF THE ORAL TRADITION

Oral testimony is historical evidence which is spoken in the first instance, rather than written down. The popular term 'oral history' is somewhat misleading because no single source, whether spoken or written, can constitute 'history' in the true sense of the word, which, by definition, is an amalgamation of evidence rather than a reliance on any single area of information. In the last twenty years much bad 'oral history' has been written without recourse to documentary information, a development which has played its part in raising the suspicions of many 'serious' historians towards the use of oral testimony in general. The group which interviews a dozen aged mill workers from Macclesfield and then feels competent to break into print with a pamphlet on 'The Cheshire Silk Industry' rarely does itself much credit and only succeeds in driving further and deeper the wedge between the 'professional' and the 'amateur' in local history. Yet such ventures have been attempted and continue to be attempted by 'oral history' enthusiasts.[1]

More sensible is the approach adopted by those excellent historians of the First World War, Martin Middlebrook and Lyn Macdonald. Middlebrook and Macdonald have discovered the central role which oral testimony can play in unfolding the events of the recent past, yet they use the reminiscences of soldiers, nurses and civilian workers as part of a framework of history which also embraces more conventional documentary sources.[2] And here lies the secret of their success. Oral testimony is extremely important in many areas of study, both local and national, but it should not be permitted to achieve a dominance it does not deserve.

Over the years people have recorded their reminiscences in many ways and I discount, for the purposes of this booklet, diaries and autobiographical memoirs, important though they are.[3] The collection of oral data is much more ancient than many people realise, and its origins in Western European society are extremely difficult to establish with any certainty. In pre-Roman times, when most Western cultures were still illiterate, legends and stories were passed on within tribes by word of mouth. Tacitus, speaking of the Germans in the first century AD, wrote:

> In their ancient songs, their only form of recorded history, the Germans celebrate the earth-born god Tuisto ... Hercules, among others, is said to have visited them, and they chant his praises before those of other heroes on their way into battle ... Ulysses, too, in those long and fabled wanderings of his, is thought by some to have reached this ocean, visited the German lands and founded and named Asciburgium, a place still inhabited today on the banks of the Rhine ... I am not disposed either to sustain or refute such assertions by evidence: my readers may believe or disbelieve of their own discretion.[4]

In his last sentence Tacitus, by his emphasis on 'evidence' (and he means *written* evidence), clearly places himself in the tradition of classical historical scholarship with all its suspicion of folk tales and myths. Yet these were the life blood of an illiterate society and were tremendously important in establishing the identity of any particular group or tribe. The people who were the custodians of these myths — bards and priests — assumed a special importance because of their knowledge. Even today in West Africa the 'griot' fulfils a very similar role, as Alex Haley discovered when he set out on the quest to rediscover his 'roots' amongst the Mandinga.[5]

After the fall of the Roman empire Bede recalls the continued importance of the bardic tradition in the person of Caedmon, a seventh century monk of Whitby:

> In this monastery of Whitby there lived a brother whom God's grace made remarkable. So skilful was he in composing religious and devotional songs, that he could quickly turn whatever passages of scripture were explained to him into delightful and moving poetry in his own English tongue ... And although he followed a secular occupation until well advanced in years, he had never learned anything about poetry; indeed whenever all those present at a feast took it in turns to sing and entertain the company, he would get up from the table and go home directly he saw the harp approaching him ... The abbess was delighted that God had given such grace to the man, and advised him to abandon secular life and adopt the monastic state. And when she had admitted him into the community as a brother, she ordered him to be instructed in the events of sacred history. So Caedmon stored up in his memory all that he had learned, and often meditating on it, turned it into such melodious verse that his delightful renderings turned his instructors into his audience.[6]

The quotation is revealing, not least because Bede is describing Anglo-Saxon England in the same terms as

A True Tale of *ROBIN HOOD.*

Or, A Brief Touch of the Life and Death of that re-
nowned Outlaw *Robert* Earl of *Huntington,* vulgar-
ly called *Robin Hood,* who lived and dyed in A.D.
1198. being the 9th. year of the Reign of King
Richard the Firſt, commonly called *Richard Cœur
de Lyon.*

Carefully collected out of the trueſt Writers of our
Engliſh Chronicles : And publiſhed for the ſatisfa-
ction of thoſe who deſire truth from falſhood.

By *Martin Parker.*

Printed for *J. Clark.*, *W. Thackeray*, and
near *Weſt-Smithfield*. 1687.

Frontispiece of *A True Tale of Robin Hood* published in 1687. Although
Robin emerged, essentially, from the oral tradition, later authors were
anxious to bestow upon him a bogus historical authenticity suggesting
that their data was 'collected out of the truest writers of our English
chronicles'.

Tacitus used for Germany. He brings out several important elements: the storing up of memories as verse; the sharing of these stories as a form of recreation; the gifted nature of those individuals entrusted with the task of transmission (the feats of memory alone must have been prodigious, quite apart from the 'melodious verse' and 'delightful renderings'). It did not matter very much whether the theme was sacred or profane. That was the way in which much of the popular culture of the Celts and Saxons was transmitted.

Despite the growth of an increasingly literate society as the Middle Ages progressed, it would be reasonable to suppose that much of the history and entertainment of the majority of people remained in this traditional framework. In the fifteenth century, with the advent of increased literacy and printing, many ancient ballads, drawn originally from the oral tradition, made their first appearance on the written page. The tales of Robin Hood and King Arthur are classic examples of this, a form of 'history' which undoubtedly had a long pedigree before the form in which it first became generally known. As might be expected, these developments did something to weaken the oral tradition, but it never disappeared. Britain became a 'literate' society only in the twentieth century, and before the advent of mass education most poor families related more readily to traditional spoken folk tales than they did to the book learning of the middle class.

The survival of folk customs, such as 'soul-caking', is a good example of this. As late as the nineteenth century villagers in many parts of the country kept All Souls Day, or its Eve, by 'souling' from house to house, which involved the singing of traditional songs and the eating of special cakes called soul-cakes. In Shropshire a ditty was sung:

A Soule-cake, a Soule-cake,
Have mercy on all Christen soules for a Soule-cake.

The custom represents a clear link, in terms of popular culture, with the recital of prayers for the dead in purgatory which was outlawed as 'superstitious' during the Protestant Reformation in the sixteenth century. Taking it back even further, the custom may well stem from the ancient Celtic New Year festival (originally celebrated in November) as part of which the dead were believed to rise from their graves and return, briefly, to the earth.[7] The soul-cakers of the Victorian era were linked with these primitive roots entirely by the power and resilience of the spoken word, but they were moving in a cultural twilight zone which increasingly was regarded as eccentric, the preserve of ignorant and superstitious country folk. Few people had the foresight of Cecil Sharp or Percy Grainger who, in the early twentieth century, spent much time and effort collecting up the last remnants of this fragile and rapidly dying culture.[8]

Alongside a popular culture of stories, ballads and songs must be set the more deliberate and structured attempts of professional historians to use the spoken word as a means of augmenting their researches. Speaking to people who participated in great events was stock-in-trade to well connected Romans such as Tacitus and Suetonius, and it was a trend that carried over into the history writing of the Middle Ages. When John de Schalby commenced his history of the Bishops of Lincoln in the early fourteenth century, he drew what evidence he could from the older canons of the Cathedral who had actually known the men he was writing about. Polydore Vergil, writing the 'official' history of the reign of Henry VII, had frequent interviews with key figures such as the Earl of Oxford who had fought at the battle of East Stoke in 1487.[9] This was the use of oral testimony in a very modern sense, though it is often hidden from the reader by lack of formal acknowledgements or references.

But few historians before the twentieth century bothered to cross the social divide and solicit the views of ordinary people about the present or the recent past. An exception was William Harrison who in his *Description of England*, first published in 1577, includes the following remarkable passage:

> There are old men yet dwelling in the village where I remain which have noted three things marvellously altered in England within their sound remembrance, and other three things too too much increased. One is the multitude of chimneys lately erected, whereas in their young days there were not above two or three ... The second is the great .. amendment of lodging, for (said they) our fathers, yea, and we ourselves also, have lien full oft upon straw pallets, or rough mats covered only with sheet, under coverlets made of dagswain or hap-harlots (I use their own terms), and a good round log under their heads instead of a bolster or pillow ... Pillows (said they) were thought meet only for women in childbed ... The third thing they tell of is the exchange of vessel, as of treen platters into pewter, and wooden spoons into silver or tin.[10]

Harrison's greybeards went on to provide more detail, particularly of social changes they disapproved of, but by any standard it is a remarkable judgment of the sixteenth century. Chimneys, beds and tableware are highlighted as the most remarkable features of the age — no mention is made of kings or queens, the huge impact of the Reformation, or the opening up of overseas empires. Moreover, Harrison proves himself to be a faithful collector of oral data because he records the exact words used by the old men ('dagswain' and 'hap-harlots') even when, apparently, he did not understand them. The account is very much a man-in-the-street's view of the period, stressing what was important to a particular individual, rather than great matters of state which were necessarily far removed from his experience and understanding. Sadly, such glimpses are rare, but for a moment Harrison draws together the world of the folk

Village Inn with Backgammon and Card Players, by Adriaen van Ostade, 1674. In environments such as this the sort of views expressed in William Harrison's *Description of England* were developed and debated by the people of Tudor and Stuart England. Reproduced by permission of the Guildhall Art Gallery, Corporation of London.

tale and the ballad and that of 'serious' scholarship and the printed word. Had more people taken his view, our understanding of pre-industrial Britain would have been much more enriched.

Historians, then, have used personal reminiscence as a source from very early times, though there has been a tendency to concentrate on the views of the rich and powerful — the shapers of great events — rather than ordinary folk whose perceptions were, generally, believed to be less relevant. Moreover, the folk tradition is still with us — most communities have their tales of hauntings, secret passages or dark deeds done in the past. Families also have their own less generalised myths passed on from one generation to the next, a decline from wealth to poverty being a common one (a theme immortalised in Thomas Hardy's *Tess of the d'Urbervilles*); but there are many more. Together these two strands comprise what might loosely be termed the oral tradition, and it was only in the middle years of the twentieth century that determined steps were taken to consolidate and preserve these extremely vulnerable threads of our heritage.

The 1960s proved to be the critical era in this respect because it saw the convergence of many trends contributing to the creation of a 'greenhouse' for the expansion of the study of the spoken word. Firstly, it was a decade of growing social awareness and left-wing views amongst the younger generation. In this atmosphere the notion of 'history from below', pioneered by the French school of history, was to become fashionable: a belief that looking at the past from a traditional standpoint of 'kings and popes' was not necessarily the only valid approach. Ordinary people too, it was believed, had something to say, and their perception of the past should be taken seriously. Secondly, the post-war period was an age of technological advance and growing mass production, and the tape recorder was becoming one of the most important pieces of leisure equipment. Fascinated by its new-fangled power, a whole generation began pirating music from the radio and television or surreptitiously placing microphones to eavesdrop on family discussions. Finally, the great prosperity of the 1960s — which enabled even working-class families to purchase gadgets such as tape recorders — led to an unprecedented expansion in Britain's universities to cope with the 'baby bulge' that followed the Second World War. A range of new universities — such as Sussex, York and Essex — meant the recruitment of a whole new generation of teachers, many of them young men and women influenced by the fashionable notions of the day and keen to find specialisms far removed from the 'stuffy' and socially retrograde work of their elders. These circumstances created a tinderbox which ignited 'oral history' as a fashionable area of study, available to the academic and non-academic alike. It was not, in itself, 'new', as some people alleged, because its constituent elements stretched back before classical civilization; what *was* new was the ready availability of the tape recorder, and a social awareness which was determined to switch the collection of oral data from élite groups and individuals to working people.

In the years following this expansive phase many individuals and institutions did much to put the collection of oral testimony on a more scientific footing. Paul Thompson of the University of Essex Department of Sociology, Ken Howarth of the North West Sound Archive, and John Widdowson of the Institute of Cultural and Linguistic Studies, University of Sheffield, are three outstanding examples.[11] But, as stated earlier, much work of an indifferent nature was also produced in the

1970s and 1980s, because equipment was available and the technique was seen by some as 'easy' — a quick means by which political or sexist points could be scored. This malpractice has done the reputation of 'oral history' no good, and to some extent we still live in its shadow today. What I hope to show in the second section is that the retrieval and proper assessment of oral evidence is far from 'easy' and that it represents a discipline similar to most other areas of research. This need not take the fun out of collecting oral data, and it will almost certainly lead to a more creditable result at the end of the day.

References

1. There are many instances of this problem, for example, S. Terkel, *Hard Times: an Oral History of the Great Depression* (Pantheon Books, 1970). The book comprises the memories of individuals, and this does not constitute a history of the American Depression.

2. See, for example, M. Middlebrook, *The Kaiser's Battle* (Penguin, 1978); L. Macdonald, *The Roses of No Man's Land* (Papermac, 1984).

3. Good examples are to be found in J. Burnet, *Useful Toil: Autobiographies of Working People from the 1820s to the 1920s* (Penguin, 1984).

4. Tacitus, *On Britain and Germany* (Penguin, 1948), pp. 102-3.

5. A. Haley, *Roots* (Hutchinson, 1977).

6. Bede, *A History of the English Church and People* (Penguin, 1955), pp. 245-7.

7. C. Hole, *A Dictionary of British Folk Customs* (Paladin, 1986), pp. 282-5.

8. J. Blacking, *A Common Sense View of all Music: Reflections on Percy Grainger's Contribution to Ethnomusicology and Music Education* (Cambridge University Press, 1987); C. Sharp, *English Folk Song: Some Conclusions* (Methuen, 1954).

9. J. H. Stawley (ed.), *The Book of John de Schalby, Canon of Lincoln 1299-1333, Concerning the Bishops of Lincoln and their Acts* (Lincoln Minster Pamphlets, 2, 1966); D. Hay (ed.), *The Anglia Historia of Polydore Vergil, 1485-1537* (Camden Society, 74, 1950).

10. W. Harrison, *The Description of England,* ed. Edelen (Folger Shakespeare Library, 1968), pp. 200-1.

11. Examples of some of the better books published over recent years are G. E. Evans, *Where Beards Wag All* (Faber and Faber, 1970); J. Vansina, *Oral Tradition* (Penguin, 1973); P. Thompson, *The Voice of the Past* (Oxford University Press, 1978); T. Lummis, *Listening to History: the Authenticity of Oral Evidence* (Hutchinson, 1987). In addition *Oral History,* Journal of the Oral History Society, carries useful monographs and reviews.

Chapter 2

HOW TO CONDUCT
AN INTERVIEW

The collection of oral testimony depends on a logical and disciplined approach to enable the historian to make the best use of the information available and pass it on to future generations. The following procedure — developed for the Nottinghamshire Oral History Project — worked well from a research and archive point of view and has been successfully commended to subsequent generations of students. Of course, if one does not wish to preserve data and simply wants to extract information for publication, a less rigorous approach can be adopted. However, this should not be encouraged, since it tends to denigrate the importance of the source material collected. It may well be of use to someone else in the future, possibly in a quite different — and unexpected — context. Moreover, the preservation of the data also allows future generations of readers and researchers to check the source material, rather than simply relying on the judgement of the individual who undertook the initial collection.

Setting a goal and finding respondents

Before one begins to collect oral testimony, it is of prime importance to set a goal so that subsequent research can be given a clear sense of direction. What do you want to know? Your quest could go in almost any direction — genealogical, occupational, or topographical, to name just three examples. It should also be circumscribed by a sense of chronology: are you researching just one or a series of incidents set into a definite chronological framework, or are you attempting to develop themes over a much longer period of time? Here are a few examples of the sort of projects which might usefully be tackled.

1)   Researching a particular theme, in a particular place over a period of years, to see what changes and developments took place; for example, most villages would have enough living respondents to give an insight into how education, as represented by the local school, altered between 1918 and the present day. The same idea could be applied to almost any social phenomenon, such as crime, diet, housing or entertainment.

2)   A topographical starting point could be adopted to trace the use and/or appearance of local buildings and landmarks in the past. This might involve walking around the area with elderly residents and a portable tape recorder, obtaining their observations about how things appeared in the past and the general process of change.

3)   In genealogical research the 'life history' approach is often most rewarding because the family historian wants to know as much about a particular individual as possible — jobs, relationships, war service and interests, for example. Here, in contrast to 1), one would try to assess an individual 'in the round' rather than extracting a particular piece of that person's life story.

4) Many projects have been built around a person's work experience by researchers interested in specific occupational themes, such as seafaring, textile working or coal mining. These might be related to a particular region or locality, but they might also be comparative — contrasting the work practices of South Wales miners with those in Durham, for example. This sort of work has the same tightness of focus as 1), but in both cases elements of 3) — the life history — tend to become involved to set work or leisure in proper context. The trick is to create a balance between one's primary objective and the supportive detail which must of necessity be brought in from time to time.

The possibilities for research are almost inexhaustible, although obviously the proposition must be a viable one, and that viability depends largely on the survival of respondents. It would be difficult today to collect much useful data on the Great War or the General Strike — events which are quickly slipping from living memory — and urban topographical study is sometimes made difficult by the rapid turnover of population in recent years. People are the raw material of the oral researcher and their existence must be guaranteed to launch any project.

How, then, are suitable candidates to be encountered? Many people ask this question with some trepidation at the start of a new venture, but it usually turns out to be less of a problem than they thought. In most communities one contact leads on to another, and in some projects there are obvious agencies to turn to for support — old persons' day centres, trade unions, military veterans' associations and many more. If all else fails, appeals on the local radio or in newspapers will usually bring in a crop of relevant responses. Once a project has been fully explained people will generally come forward to assist it, and other more reticent folk may be discovered by determined detective work as events move on. Most researchers find themselves at the end of the day with more potential respondents than they can cope with. They will not all make good interviewees and some will have to be rejected, but all offers of help should be acknowledged and a register of names built up. In an extensive project it should be politely explained to all potential helpers at the outset that it may well be some time before a member of the team makes contact with them personally. One of the tasks of the project director is to try to work out which respondents should be given priority for an interview. A simple queue is not good enough, because, inevitably, there will be those, who, on account of age and frailness, should be dealt with first. Some discreet questioning as to the state of health of the candidates at the point of initial contact can often help to resolve problems such as these.

The preliminary interview

Once a respondent has been selected, a preliminary interview should be undertaken by the researcher. This should be conducted in the respondent's own home, if possible, and without the presence of a tape recorder. Experienced interviewers are far from agreed on the sort of approach to be adopted at the preliminary. It is often stated that an over-long first encounter can damage the spontaneity of the eventual interview and perhaps deter the respondent from co-operating at all. These points should be seriously considered and the preliminary meeting organised to take account of them; but it would be difficult to conceive of a situation in which the tape recorder could be usefully introduced on the first encounter.

Local History Certificate students at Nottingham University undertaking a 'practice interview' prior to being turned loose on genuine respondents.

The object of the preliminary meeting is threefold. Firstly, it enables the researcher to establish contact with the respondent so that a relaxed and friendly interchange can take place. Avoid jumping in with historical interrogation straight away. It is important, and polite, to break the ice with general conversation and then to work round gradually to the real purpose of the meeting. Allow yourself plenty of time. Many elderly people do not receive many visitors and will make the most of the opportunity to tell you all about their gardens, their grandchildren or the whims of their pets. In any event listen patiently, because the rapport and confidence built up in this way will shine through in the final interview. Secondly, the researcher must steer the conversation on to the real purpose of the meeting and begin to make some sort of assessment of what contribution the respondent

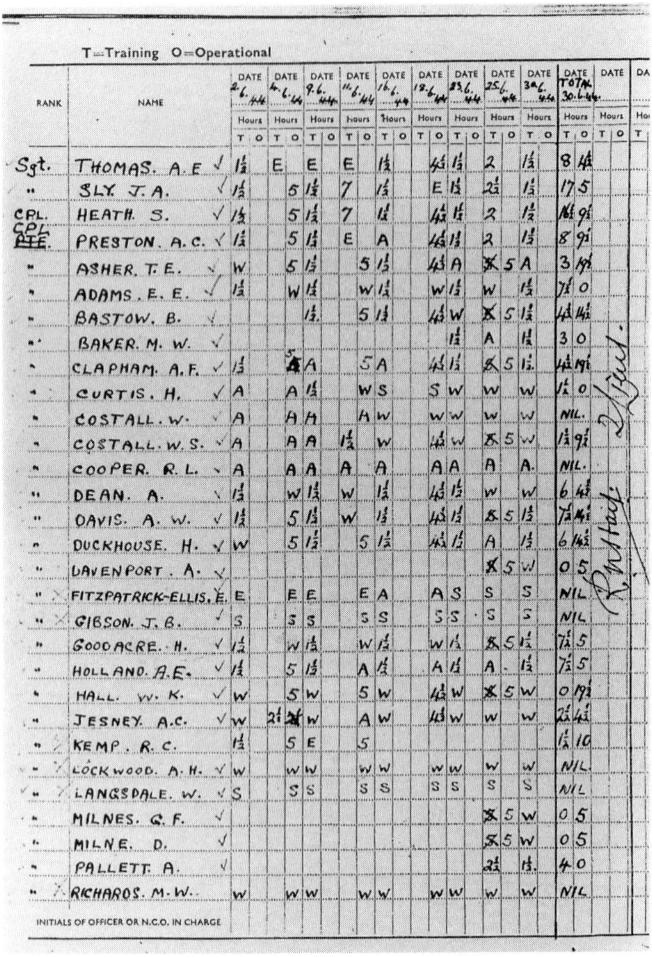

T=Training O=Operational

RANK	NAME	DATE 2.6.44 Hours		DATE 4.6.44 Hours		DATE 9.6.44 Hours		DATE 11.6.44 Hours		DATE 16.6.44 Hours		DATE 18.6.44 Hours		DATE 23.6.44 Hours		DATE 25.6.44 Hours		DATE 30.6.44 Hours		DATE TOTAL 30.6.44 Hours		DATE Hours		DA Hours
		T	O	T	O	T	O	T	O	T	O	T	O	T	O	T	O	T	O	T	O	T	O	T
Sgt.	THOMAS. A. E ✓	1½		E		E		E		1½			4½	1½		2		1½		8	4½			
"	SLY. J. A. ✓	1½			5	1½		7		1½			E	1½		2½		1½		17	5			
CPL.	HEATH. S. ✓	1½			5	1½		7		1½			4½	1½		2		1½		16½	9½			
CPL ~~PTE.~~	PRESTON. A. C. ✓	1½			5	1½		E		A			4½	1½		2		1½		8	9½			
"	ASHER. T. E. ✓	W			5	1½			5	1½			4½	A		~~5~~	5	A		3	19½			
"	ADAMS. E. E. ✓	1½			W	1½			W	1½			W	1½		W		1½		7½	0			
"	BASTOW. B. ✓					1½.			5	1½			4½	W		~~5~~	5	1½		4½	14½			
"	BAKER. M. W. ✓													1½		A		1½		3	0			
"	CLAPHAM. A. F. ✓	1½			5 ~~4~~	A			5	A			4½	1½		~~5~~	5	1½.		4½	19½			
"	CURTIS. H. ✓	A			A	1½			W	S			S	W		W		W		1½	0			
"	COSTALL. W. ✓	A			A	A			A	W			W	W		W		W		NIL.				
"	COSTALL. W. S. ✓	A			A	A		1½		W			4½	W		~~5~~	5	W		1½	9½			
"	COOPER. R. L. ✓	A			A	A		A		A			A	A		A		A.		NIL.				
"	DEAN. A. ✓	1½			W	1½		W		1½			4½	1½		W		W		6	4½			
"	DAVIS. A. W. ✓	1½			5	1½		W		1½			4½	1½		~~5~~	5	1½		7½	4½			
"	DUCKHOUSE. H. ✓	W			5	1½			5	1½			4½	1½		A		1½		6	14½			
"	DAVENPORT. A. ✓															~~5~~	5	W		0	5			
"	FITZPATRICK-ELLIS. E. ✓	E			E	E			E	A			A	S		S		S		NIL				
"	GIBSON. J. B. ✓	S			S	S			S	S			S	S		S		S		NIL				
"	GOODACRE. H. ✓	1½			W	1½			W	1½			W	1½		~~5~~	5	1½		7½	5			
"	HOLLAND. A. E. ✓	1½			5	1½			A	1½			A	1½		A	.	1½		7½	5			
"	HALL. W. K. ✓	W			5	W			5	W			4½	W		~~5~~	5	W		0	19½			
"	JESNEY. A. C. ✓	W		2½	~~2½~~	W			A	W			4½	W		W		W		2½	4½			
"	KEMP. R. C.	1½			5	E			5											1½	10			
"	LOCKWOOD. A. H. ✓	W			W	W			W	W			W	W		W		W		NIL.				
"	LANGSDALE. W. ✓	S			S	S			S	S			S	S		S		S		NIL				
"	MILNES. G. F. ✓															~~5~~	5	W		0	5			
"	MILNE. D. ✓															~~5~~	5	W		0	5			
"	PALLETT. A. ✓															2½		1½.		4	0			
"	RICHARDS. M. W.	W			W	W			W	W			W	W		W		W		NIL				
INITIALS OF OFFICER OR N.C.O. IN CHARGE																								

Jack Sly of Keyworth, formerly a Sergeant in the Home Guard, was able to produce substantial documentation relating to the volunteer forces in World War Two. Here the Home Guard Register of Hours of Attendance (Army Book 527) illustrates the time that the men of 'A' Company, No 1 Platoon, 2nd Notts Home Guard, spent on their military duties in June 1944.

could make to the project. Do his or her experiences match up with the parameters of your research? Does his or her voice and memory seem to be reasonably unimpaired? Is the person physically and emotionally strong enough to sustain an interview? If so, how long might it go on for? These are some of the issues which should be considered, and it would be sensible to take notes, particularly on matters of fact which might help later in the framing of the interview proper.

The researcher should always enquire whether or not the respondent has any photographs, documents or newspaper cuttings which might illuminate the theme of the meeting: if these are not immediately to hand they might be looked out in readiness for the next encounter. Supplementary information of this sort is invaluable in providing documentary back-up for an interview. Make it clear that if anything is to hand, or can be found, it will not be copied without permission and that the originals will be returned to the owner.

Finally, the researcher needs to make some mental assessment of the suitability of the respondent's home for conducting an interview. Is there an electrical socket to hand and is there any objection to its use? Is there undue noise from traffic, hissing gas fires or noisy pets? Is there an 'interruption problem' with husband, wife or neighbour chiming in from time to time with unwelcome observations? If all or any of these problems exist, it may be worth discreetly enquiring about the possibility of another room for the interview or conducting it at a time when relative privacy can be guaranteed. These are important practical issues and the preliminary interview is the proper time to work through them.

When you leave, thank the respondent for his or her time and let it be known that you will be in touch again soon. Do not make a date for a final interview unless you are *very* confident that your respondent will be suitable. If you are working as part of a team this will probably be a decision for your project director in any case.

Assessment and research

The period following the preliminary meeting is vital, and the first question to consider is whether or not to go ahead with the respondent in question. Rejection could be based on any of the criteria noted above, or indeed on any other good reason observed by the researcher. In this event the respondent should be sent a letter simply thanking him or her for their contribution to the project — and a contribution *will* have been made even if a person is not considered suitable for a full interview. Rejection rates will vary, and are dictated by many factors — the amount of time and money available to the researcher, the number of alternative respondents to be approached, and the criteria set by the research team. The important thing to remember is that not everyone is a good interviewee, and the possibility of pruning should be carefully considered at this stage of the exercise.

Assuming the interview is to go ahead, the researcher must now prepare an interview schedule and this takes more time than is sometimes thought. First, some supplementary research must be conducted to provide a context for the areas highlighted in the preliminary. If the interview is to be with a cabinet maker or dairy maid, for example, it is necessary to have some rudimentary knowledge of these tasks so that questioning can be relatively well informed and not rooted in total ignorance. A well stocked library should provide some leads here in the form of books, pamphlets or newspapers, and the growing preponderence of tape archives might afford useful comparative interviews. Visual prompts such as old photographs, which might assist the respondent, can sometimes be located and copied during the research period. During the Nottinghamshire project one of our research assistants located a cricket bat maker who had worked for the famous firm of Gunn and Moore; during her research she uncovered an old advertising photograph which featured the company's workshop. When this was set before the respondent — who had quite forgotten about it — it sparked off memories of colleagues he had worked with and some of the processes involved in cricket bat making. It proved to be an invaluable aid, and such discoveries should not for too long defy the determined researcher.

Once the background work has been done, the researcher needs to put together some sort of interview schedule. Much debate has centred around the nature of

The picture of Gunn and Moore's workshop that triggered a stream of reminiscences from a former employee of the firm. It underlines the importance of visual prompts in the collection of oral testimony.

these schedules. Some scholars favour the questionnaire approach on the grounds that it guarantees a consistency of information and irons out the inevitable differences of approach and emphasis between different interviewers. This may be so, but its weakness is that it is impersonal and inflexible and assumes a lack of knowledge and sensitivity on the part of the interviewer. If an interviewer is well chosen — and the principal requirements here are warmth of personality and an ability to communicate intelligently with others — it should be possible to abandon the inflexibility of the questionnaire while maintaining the academic integrity of the interview. The interviewer needs to work within a framework, but also requires the flexibility to branch out and explore useful tangents when and if they occur. The problem with the questionnaire is that it discourages this sort of spontaneous response from the interviewee and keeps the whole conversation on a narrow, pre-ordained track. The researcher should prepare a written agenda of questions and issues to be discussed; this will allow for some digression, but will enable the interview to be quickly put back 'on track' if things begin to get out of hand. Once this work has been completed the respondent should be contacted again, by letter or by telephone, and asked for a convenient time when a final interview may be undertaken.

Equipment

If the problem of equipment has not already been sorted out, now is the time to give some thought to the technical basis for the interview. The Nottinghamshire project used a Uher 4000 Report Monitor reel-to-reel tape recorder with free-standing microphone. This machine can function on battery or mains power and is widely used by BBC local radio. The Uher can therefore guarantee a high standard of reproduction, and it is proven to be very durable. Its disadvantage — for the private researcher — lies in its cost which to most research groups or societies is prohibitive. Some local collecting agencies are prepared to lend good quality equipment (this is certainly the case in Nottinghamshire), but failing this the researcher would be well advised to obtain the best possible machine within the budget available.

Reel-to-reel machines with free-standing microphones tend to provide a better end product, but these are becoming increasingly difficult to obtain in High Street electrical shops where the emphasis is firmly on cassette players with built-in microphones. Tape recorders of this sort do a perfectly good job if they are set up and positioned correctly, and in years to come it looks as if most oral work will have to be done with equipment of this nature. There are two golden rules. Firstly, obtain the best tape recorder and tapes that you can afford — always remembering to read the instructions very carefully! Secondly, don't be put off by the belief that your equipment might not be up to scratch. At the end of the day it is more important that the interview is *done* — albeit, maybe, on an inferior machine — than that it be done on high-quality equipment.

The interview

The recorded interview itself is obviously central to the whole process of gathering oral testimony. Like the preliminary meeting, it should be held in the respondent's home if at all possible, because a familiar environment gives people confidence and sets them at their ease. It should be held in a room which is comfortable and relatively free from interruption or sounds that will be detrimental to the recording. Some hazards to watch out for are:

1)   Background noise caused by traffic, ticking clocks, budgerigars and gas fires. These may sound innocuous enough in everyday life, but they can be annoying and intrusive on tape. Some researchers welcome background noise because of the 'local colour' it provides. Maybe a case can be made in that direction, but it does blur the audibility of tapes and makes them virtually useless if they are ever to be used in broadcasting.

2)   Echoes caused by large empty spaces. Small rooms are best for recorded interviews, but if there is no alternative to a large room it is probably wise to move into a corner near some curtains so that the sound can be absorbed by the fabric and the worst effects of echo eliminated.

It is important that both interviewer and respondent should be seated comfortably and the tape recorder positioned as unobtrusively as possible between them. The microphone (assuming it to be free-standing) should be positioned on a table or stand between interviewer and interviewee and should never be held; hand contact results in 'mike rattle' which has rendered many tapes virtually inaudible. In addition, it is important to position the microphone far enough away from the tape recorder to ensure that it does not pick up a buzz from the workings of the machine. Good results have recently been reported by modern clip-on microphones which can be attached to an overgarment or lapel. Before you begin to record, check your sound level and say a few words to be sure the equipment is working properly: there are many heart rending examples of researchers who have sat through long interviews only to find their tapes blank at the end of the exercise because of some simple problem not rectified in the early stages. Once you are positioned and the essential checks have been run, you are ready to commence recording.

In the interview the interviewer should assume an attitude of 'informed naivety'; in other words, he or she

The interview in progress: Maurice Rushby, retired head gardener of Saxondale Hospital, Nottinghamshire, talking to Susan Clayton at Flintham. Photograph, Trevor Clayton.

should be prepared to set up the right sort of questions, but to feign ignorance when it comes to their answers. An interviewer should not try to project ideas or knowledge into the interview; the task is merely that of a catalyst to encourage the respondent to speak. Never argue with your respondent even when you know he or she may be wrong on a point of fact: the interview is the respondent's forum and any errors can be compensated for later without causing feelings of ill-will or embarrassment.

Coax and encourage by the use of body language as much as possible rather than by intrusive interjections into the microphone; hands and eyes can be used to say 'come on, tell me some more', just as well as words. Sometimes, on the other hand, you might need to come to the rescue of your respondent by substituting words where he or she may have used a descriptive gesture. The interviewee may say something like 'the tool we used in the tanning trade was that long' (indicating about twelve inches with the hands). Obviously this would be lost on any listener, so it is incumbent on the interviewer to intervene quickly with a confirming statement — 'You mean about twelve inches?' The meaning is thus clarified for everyone. The essence of the interviewer's job is experience and common sense — to know when to speak and when to keep silent; when to encourage a respondent to say more and when to move a rambling monologue on to a different and more productive tack.

It is often asked how long the ideal interview should be. This is rather like the proverbial piece of string. It depends on what a person has to say. In the Nottingham- shire project our shortest interview was twenty minutes and the longest in excess of eight hours. Typically interviews tended to fall somewhere between these ex- tremes — there were many of about sixty minutes dura- tion — but if an interview does seem to be going on for a long time the interviewer must watch carefully for signs of fatigue. Some elderly people get tired easily, and recalling (sometimes traumatic) events of the past can have unexpected and dramatic effects.

If you feel that you have reached a reasonable pausing point or that you are encountering problems due to tiredness or emotional stress, it is always best to suspend the interview until another day. In longer interviews a researcher could expect to make perhaps four or five visits, and this is quite acceptable with the agreement of the respondent. On the other hand, you should never drag out an interview beyond its natural life. This can often cause resentment and a failure to understand why information, once given, has to be repeated. Once again it is a question of balance and sensitivity. Let the respondent say what needs to be said, no more and no less, and be patient enough to accept that gracefully.

After the interview, a cup of tea or coffee is often greatly appreciated by both parties, and during this final — informal — session the last tasks can be undertaken. The respondent should be reminded of your request for photographs and documents, and if these are available, and relevant, they should be removed to be copied; a signed receipt should be given if requested. It is useful if a contemporary photograph of the respondent 'at home' accompanies the tape, and this can be taken with a simple flash camera.

If you are considering publishing or broadcasting your findings at any stage, it would be wise to draw up and have signed a 'consent form' stating that the respondent has no objection to his or her memories, or voice, being used in a particular way. The law is ambiguous as to whether copyright of a recorded interview rests with the interviewer or interviewee, and for this reason it is wise to proceed with a fair degree of circumspection.

Consent forms should be drawn up with particular projects in view, but they could, for example, contain clauses which restrict publication or broadcasting for a certain number of years or until after a person's death. In case of doubt a solicitor should certainly be consulted. In most instances this would not apply, but some interviews inevitably go 'near the bone' and if spread abroad may lay interviewer and interviewee open to an accusation of libel or slander.

It is unwise during this winding down process to play back the tape to the respondent, except, perhaps, the tiniest snippet to make sure that the recording has come through. People sometimes ask that this be done, but it should be politely declined. The reason is that many people are dissatisfied with the sound of their own voices on tape, or indeed with the content of the interview: they often think of ways in which it could be improved. This is sometimes true, but it is not the point of the exercise. Tell them that they would be very welcome to hear the tape at some future date and that — funds permitting — a copy might be provided for them to keep. In practice very few will take up this offer.

Finally, the interviewee should be thanked for his or her time and the use of their home. All respondents should be contacted at a later date with a formal letter of thanks, pointing out how their particular contribution has helped the study in hand.

Storage, analysis and transcription

It would be tempting to believe that the job of the researcher is now over. On the contrary, the most time-consuming element of the task is about to begin. First, the new tape needs to be stored in a place where it is safe and free from the various hazards which threaten its existence. And there are more of these than might at first seem apparent. Storage temperature and humidity levels must be moderate, and care must be taken to avoid direct sunlight. The accumulation of dirt must be minimised by the careful closure of doors and boxes. Tapes that remain unused for a long period of time should be run through occasionally to minimise the risk of 'print through', or accidental transfer of material to the underside of the tape.

Most alarming of all, perhaps, are the risks posed by unexpected magnetic fields which can totally erase the sound from tapes; things to look out for here are steel shelves (always use wood), loudspeakers, television sets, lifts, bridges, and hot water radiators orientated north/ south. Maintaining a distance of at least two or three feet from some of these objects should negate the worst effects. If the researcher is seriously worried about the possibility of loss or damage, a copy should be made as soon as possible and stored elsewhere. The copy tape, rather than the original, can then be used for the various playbacks which will be necessary in the task of assessment and transcription. Where the original recording is made on reel-to-reel tape it will probably be more convenient to make a copy on a cassette because these are, in many ways, more convenient and less liable to damage.

As soon as possible after the interview, while the events are still fresh in the mind, the interviewer must play through the tape and complete an analysis sheet based on it. The analysis sheet provides a written record of the circumstances of the interview and an immediate guide to the contents of the tape. This need not be very detailed, and should provide a note of tape footage readings coupled with 'key words' describing briefly what is being said — effectively, a précis of the interview. Thus, a researcher interested in 'education' or 'trade union membership' should in theory be able to gain quick, though somewhat rough and ready, access to the tape. It is important to provide this minimal service to the user at once, since more detailed transcription and indexing could perhaps take months, or even years, to complete. But these must be the ultimate goals.

All tapes should be transcribed in full as near to the original diction as can be managed. This is best done by an experienced typist using audio equipment with a foot control, and it should take account of dialectical spellings, the inevitable 'ums' and 'ers' and pauses in the narrative. No attempt should be made to 'clean up' the text, tempting though this may be at times. The job of the audio-typist is exacting and time consuming and is never wholly successful since there are often words that can never be clearly deciphered. The Nottingham project worked on a ratio of one hour of playing time to six hours of transcription time.

Transcription is an exercise which is justified for two reasons. Firstly, the survival of magnetic tape over a long period of time is still an unknown quantity, and a transcription ensures that the information will survive even if the tape, for some reason, perishes. Secondly, many historians and researchers prefer to work from transcripts than from tapes; this has something to do with the nature of conventional academic training which still places emphasis on documents over and above the spoken word, but nevertheless it is a tradition which exists and should be catered for. In matters of doubt the tape can always be referred to to clarify inflexions and nuances that may not be evident from the transcript. Tape and transcript should thus be used together, but experience proves that the transcript, where it exists, is usually the first and quickest way in to an interview.

Audio typists transcribing interviews undertaken during the Notting-hamshire Oral History Project. Despite its unglamorous nature, this behind-the-scenes work was vital to the success of the project.

Finally, a detailed index should be drawn up high-lighting names, places, occupations or any other aspects thought to be relevant. When a tape collection grows to a considerable size the index becomes a huge undertak-ing in its own right.

It is easy to underestimate the importance of these rather unglamorous tasks which need to be undertaken when a new tape returns to base. There are researchers who have amassed hundreds of tapes, representing thou-sands of hours of playing time, but through neglect of this fundamental infrastructure have no way of accessing them. This is obviously unsatisfactory from everyone's point of view. Once the freshness of an interview fades in the memory it is exceedingly difficult to revive it without recourse to a set of written searching aids. Even if a group or individual does not possess audio-typing equipment, a real effort should be made to undertake the transcription work on a make-do-and-mend basis. Quite successful results can be obtained by using a simple cassette player and typewriter, though wear and tear on the 'pause' button can become somewhat excessive!

Chapter 3

THE USE AND ABUSE
OF ORAL TESTIMONY

Having made a recording and undertaken the necessary
supplementary work, the researcher must inevitably ask
how reliable a source has been created and what use it is
likely to be to the present and, indeed, future generations.
Clearly, there are difficulties with oral testimony, just as
there are with all other sources, and for this reason tapes
and transcripts must be approached with a degree of
caution. Even when a respondent has been 'screened'
during the preliminary process there are sometimes
problems stemming from age and attitude coming
through on the final tape. Age can lead to forgetfulness
and a tendency to get things mixed up; while an old
person's memories of youth and recent events are often
detailed and factually correct, those of his or her middle
years are frequently muddled. Many researchers have
remarked how an elderly person can often recall quite
vividly the events of childhood, school, and the first
months of work or marriage, while subsequent years —
prior to retirement — merge into a blur. This says a good
deal about the nature of human memory, but also about
our society which tends to trap people of a certain social
stratum into depressingly boring tasks, much of which
they seem to expunge from their conscious awareness.
Memory can play tricks, and points considered of interest
by the researcher may not have been remembered by the

respondent because they were not considered important.
Dates seem to be more vulnerable than people and places
in this respect, and it is important to remember how
chronology is often linked with geography or personal
relationship in 'popular memory'; an event might be
described as happening 'soon after Aunty Mary got
married', for example, or 'in the year we had the holiday
at Torquay'. Some well-informed probing or math-
ematical calculations by the interviewer may be a help in
this respect, but certainly the clarity and cohesion of a
respondent's reminiscences will rarely match up to the
ideal.

Dishonesty and prejudice are other problems, more
intractable, perhaps, than mere forgetfulness. Some
people — often members of political parties or trade
unions — see the prospect of an interview as their last
chance to make their mark on history, and consequently
many partisan points might be made either overtly or
covertly. Some of these can be instantly seen through for
what they are — and they should not be discouraged
since they are part of that person's individuality, something always to be respected and amplified on tape — but
others, particularly those hidden in the distant past, are
more difficult to detect and penetrate. The last survivor
of a company boardroom or a regimental mess is in a
unique position to influence the history of that organisation as he or she thinks fit; with all sources of contradic-
tion gone, colleagues might be lionised or lampooned at
will with no right of reply. A good example of the way in
which persistent misinformation can blossom into an
historical orthodoxy in its own right is the case of the
nineteenth-century Durham coalowner, the Marquis of
Londonderry, who died in 1854. Despite the fact that he
died in the high Victorian period, I can well remember
old miners in the 1960s declaiming about the evils of this
man, particularly how he would order the flooding of

seams full of men in order to rescue valuable machinery following mine disasters. In fact, research undertaken in the 1970s indicated that Londonderry was a fairly benevolent employer and that much of the traditional 'history' was somewhat dubious. Evidently these stories were invented and kept alive by union activists keen to maintain a wedge between workforce and management.[1]

The perpetuation of such myths is an interesting enough phenomenon in its own right, but it clearly takes us into the realms of folklore rather than history in the true sense of the word. And dishonesty does not necessarily take the form of political bigotry. Some people are still extremely snobbish and might create an impression that their family was better off — or, conversely, worse off — than in fact it was. The woman who described her father as a solicitor when in fact he was a county court bailiff is a typical example; many of these statements have a grain of truth in them (as in the case of Lord Londonderry), but they are not strictly reliable as historical data. Similarly, events such as bankruptcies, illegitimacies, or criminal convictions — conceived of by older people as a 'disgrace' — might be deliberately withheld or euphemistically skated around with vague statements. There is no obvious solution to these problems of inaccuracy. Some details could perhaps be cross-checked against material in books, documents or newspapers, or with other oral testimony, if it exists. However, at the end of the day the researcher must accept an interview as a unique and very personal view of the past with all of the strengths and weaknesses that this implies. A knowledge of the respondent's personality, built up in the preliminary interview, should provide a shrewd researcher with a 'feel' for the situation and a view as to whether a particular person is deliberately attempting to mislead or is holding back information.

Having noted these reservations, what are the advantages of oral testimony over and above more conventional documentary sources? Sometimes, of course, it gives us information about matters not normally discussed in documents and in these instances oral testimony can provide our primary information. Important decisions have always been taken by people verbally either over dinner or in one of those quasi-secret societies such as the Foresters or the Freemasons: anyone who had read the minutes of a committee meeting, and compared them with what was said around the table, will understand this point, and many decisions are taken without even this minimal form of recording. This is especially true in the case of groups or organisations who have no tradition of written records, whose records are likely to be lost due to lack of statutory protection, or for whom it was dangerous or undesirable to leave written records. The criminal fraternity is a case in point, and in 1984 a BBC Radio Nottingham project attempted to unlock some of the secrets of the 'The Nottingham Underworld'. What came out of this very quickly was the sharp divergence between the written accounts of newspapers and law courts and the views and motives of those people on the 'wrong' side of the law who were only being heard because somebody bothered to speak to them. The usual caveats about prejudice and special pleading applied — more so than usual in this case, perhaps — but the exercise was, nevertheless, worth undertaking as the only way of illuminating a dark corner of our recent social history.

Another similar example concerns the National Unemployed Workers' Movement which was active in the 1930s and was regarded by the government of the day as subversive and revolutionary, if not directly criminal. Although the leader of the movement, Wal Hannington, attempted to make clear the aims and objectives of the NUWM in a number of publications from 1935 onwards, newspaper reports were inevitably hostile with much talk of Bolshevik infiltration and unpatriotic behaviour. It was, therefore, especially interesting in the Nottinghamshire Oral History Project to be able to speak to some local activists to see exactly what the movement did, and to ascertain whether the more extravagant accusations levelled against it were true. From interviews conducted with former members, it appeared that the main thrust of the organisation was directed towards peaceful protest and an attempt to educate people in how

Harry Davis, pictured soon after his interview in 1982. Harry was born in South Wales in 1897 and fought in the Great War. Having moved to Nottingham in the 1930s he became an activist with the National Unemployed Workers' Movement and he provided a good deal of valuable information about its activities.

to use the rudimentary state benefit system of the time, just as Hannington had argued. This perception would have been blurred had it not been for interviews conducted fifty years after the events under discussion.[2] And in some of these, rich details emerged; accounts, for example, of the planning underpinning the protest marches, and of the songs that were sung by the men on their way to lobby Parliament during the dark days of the depression. It is important to emphasise that facts and perceptions such as these would often be entirely lost but for the deliberate seeking out of respondents and the recording of their testimony. So as a means of monitoring minority experience — especially that which conflicts with the dominant middle class and patriarchal attitudes of early twentieth century Britain—oral testimony has an important role to play. Indeed, if we chose to examine a comparatively recent phenomenon — such as the riots involving the black community in Mosside or Toxteth in the 1980s or the protests of the Acanite Tribe over road building in the 1990s — the crucial significance of the interview would soon assert itself.

Less dramatically than in the closed world of the company boardroom or the twilight zone of the under-privileged, oral testimony can give us an important view into the lives of ordinary working people and the sort of society in which they lived. Two areas, perhaps, are of special interest here. The first is the way in which practice on the shop floor or in the home often deviated from theoretical rules set down in the text books or by management. The second is how it *felt* to be employed in a coal mine or to be a woman with the responsibility of keeping a large family on a very low income. These considerations, important to the broad mass of people, have only ever been of secondary importance in archive sources, with their constant emphasis on matters of general administration and accounting. Examples of both of these themes are numerous and have been documented in all parts of the country. Despite the introduction of compulsory secondary education in 1880, many country schools were virtually empty at harvest time when working children were still a vital source of income for poor families and a necessary source of labour for the farmers. Since parents needed the money and the farmers sat on the school boards — and the children mostly regarded harvesting as good fun, in any case — the schoolteachers were left alone in their frustration. Similarly, despite a series of Acts restricting child labour in factories in the nineteenth century and the establishment of a factory inspectorate, stories abound of these sober-sided gentlemen being hoodwinked by overlookers hiding small children in lofts when inspectors turned up unannounced in the mill yard.

A group of workers at the Stewton brick and tile works, near Louth, Lincolnshire, in June 1920. The huge stack of clay field drains tells us something about agricultural priorities in the county in the early twentieth century: the history of the men who produced them remains to be wirtten.

If the reality of a child's life at the turn of the century was often at odds with what well meaning Parliamentarians intended it to be, adults too led lives the details of which might conflict with what we have been led to believe or with the standards of our own times. It is through oral testimony that we can learn of the sad reality of working life for many men and women before the Second World War: the harsh working conditions of the migrant East Anglian maltsters at Burton-on-Trent vividly evoked in George Ewart Evans' book *Where Beards Wag All*; the keeping of domestic poultry in city centre back-to-backs and the appalling smells connected with urban overcrowding; the power of charge hands and foremen in many mills and factories to hire and fire workers, to determine their jobs and to organise their payment; and, linked with this, the dangerous short cuts which were often taken by workers on 'piecework' risking life and limb and defying regulations in order to take home a little more money at the end of the week. None of this would come out in company records — much of it, indeed, would be deliberately suppressed.

Perhaps even more important than information relating to happenings in the home or workplace is the insight that oral testimony can give as to how these situations imposed themselves on the feelings and attitudes of the individuals involved. One golden rule for the collector of oral testimony must be: don't just go for the facts; find out what it felt like too. To understand how situations moulded attitudes — and attitudes in their turn imposed themselves on situations — is an important function of the social historian and an area in which the oral practitioner is particularly able to contribute. Examples abound of the feelings of complacency and confidence which came with wealth, and the dejection and desperation born of poverty. The mass of working people whose lot fell within neither of these extremes adjusted to their lives as best they could, their attitudes moulded by family tradition or the pronouncements of preachers and the popular media. Jill Liddington's review of *Reminiscences of a Bradford Mill Girl* in the *Oral History Journal* brings out well the impact that starting work had on the mind of one twelve year old half-timer:

> As Maggie woke up in the morning, her thoughts raced ahead of her: 'This was it! Today I started work: soon I would be bringing a wage home, and all my mother's money troubles would be over. I was twelve and grown up. I hurried downstairs'. Three-pence a week spending money out of her wages sounded great. She had never had more than a penny a week before. But soon the harsh reality of mill life began to dawn: long hours, not-so-high wages, unfamiliar dangers. Her plaits must be tucked into the back of her pinny or they would get caught in the rollers which 'would fetch your scalp off as clean as a whistle'. George the overlooker 'would walk down the aisles .. waving his alley strap and cracking it on the floor .. I was always afraid of it. I suppose that is why it cracked so often near me'. And her leisurely hours of childhood reading had gone, for she had school in the afternoon and had to be in bed by eight. 'Off you go to bed, you're a worker now', her mother told her. 'Don't pick that book up, you've no time for that now'. Threepence was a lot to spend, but she began to wonder at what cost it was acquired. Maggie's detailed descriptions of mill life should certainly be prescribed text for any historian wanting to understand Britain's once flourishing textile industry.[3]

If the growing feeling of disillusionment is the underlying theme here, it should not be imagined that all workers were dissatisfied with their jobs or with the rewards they received. A BBC Radio Nottingham series broadcast in 1986 to celebrate Industry Year questioned, amongst others, women employed in the big city factories of Boots and Players. Both firms paid quite well and adopted a pleasantly paternalistic attitude to their employees, enabling the Players girls — known locally as 'the Angels' — to dress well, splash out at the sales, and enjoy comfortable holidays, albeit at the cost of their annual bonus. But there was a distinct feeling — both amongst the factory girls and the townspeople in general — that the two sets of workers were very different. Connie Mead, who worked as a leaf stripper at Players recalled that:

> Players Angels in those days were known as the Shockers — they were ladies of doubtful integrity, you know. And they were, some of them, let's be honest. If you worked at Players they used to look at you and think you were a bit of all right, sort of thing.[4]

By contrast, on the other side of town, Winn Beuzeval worked in the Boots factory, a more tightly regulated and altogether more respectable regime:

> I remember my parents being very proud of the fact that I had got on at Boots ... If you went at half past eight rather than eight o'clock that was a leg up in the social structure ... I thought that Boots had probably got one over Players anyway. There was a little bit of antagonism almost. If you went to the Palais or anything, 'Oh well, snooty madam, she works so-and-so, you know'. It was quite fun.[5]

Attitudes such as these are amongst the most important and illuminating data to be recovered by the collector of oral testimony, and, combined with more prosaic information about the workplace and the home, they build a picture of a working-class society much more complex than we are sometimes led to believe. It was the sort of society so ably described for Salford in Robert Roberts' book *The Classic Slum* but reflected in innumerable urban ghettos from Glasgow to Bristol. From interviews we begin to learn that working people had a wide range of pay structures; that their prosperity varied from time to time; and that they had their own internal rivalries. Many people did not enjoy the full benefit of governmental assistance or protective legislation (such as it was), yet political involvement was certainly less than some activists would have us believe. This is partly because most people's horizons were still remarkably narrow by modern standards, the main foci of life being local institutions such as pubs and corner shops. Other historians will debate these issues at length in other places, but here the importance of oral testimony in the whole information gathering process must be emphasised. It is only the voice of ordinary men and women that has opened up this area of debate and, as a result, is giving us a better understanding of the society in which we live. And, of course, this example is just one amongst many. Although we have tended to gravitate towards examples drawn from twentieth-century urban communities, many other areas could profit from having the same sort of techniques applied and similar questions asked — life in the countryside; in the armed forces; or in the colonies. Many more historical and sociological sacred cows could similarly succumb to the inroads of the tape recorder; as individuals speak out, so the old and comforting generalisations become increasingly difficult to uphold.

Finally, two further benefits of oral testimony need to be mentioned, neither of them directly involved with the

question of historical interpretation. The first is the
possible acquisition of bye-products such as documents,
photographs and artefacts relevant to the respondent, or
perhaps of wider interest. The assessing and copying of
these has already been discussed, and originals — if of
sufficient interest — could always be directed towards
local museums or archive collections, perhaps as a be-
quest after the owner's death. By entering a person's
home in a position of trust, the responsible researcher can
work for the future benefit of history and the community
in all sorts of ways. Secondly, recorded tapes have a
linguistic value quite independent of their historical
relevance, and in an age in which local dialects are
disappearing the collector of oral testimony is sometimes
inadvertently in the vanguard of the movement for their
preservation. Historians rarely possess the talents of
linguists — Professor John Widdowson of the University
of Sheffield perhaps comes closest to marrying the two —
yet the historian must surely be aware of unusual words
and phrases or inflexions of speech.[6] Even when the
proper interpretation of this is left to someone else, the
researcher has nevertheless forged the first vital link in
the chain, by ensuring the *survival* of the data.

References

1. For differing perspectives on the Marquis of Londonderry, see
    A. J. Heesom, 'Coal, Class and Education', *Past and Present*, 90
    (1981) and R. Colls, *The Pitman of the Northern Coalfield; Work,
    Culture and Protest, 1790-1850* (Manchester University Press,
    1987).

2. U(niversity of) N(ottingham) C(entre for) L(ocal) H(istory),
    Tape Collection (TC), No. 26. (Mr H. Davis). For the writings
    of Wal Hannington on the NUWM, see *Unemployed Struggles*
    (1935), *The Problem of the Distressed Areas* (1937) and *Ten Lean
    Years* (1940).

3. Jill Liddington, Review of 'Reminiscences of a Bradford Mill Girl', *Oral History*, 10, No. 1 (1982), p. 69. A graphic picture of working-class life in the early twentieth century is provided in A. Hewins (ed.), *The Dillen: Memories of a Man of Stratford-upon-Avon* (Elm Tree Books, 1981). For a recent academic study, see T. Lummis, *Occupation and Society: East Anglian Fishermen, 1880-1914* (Cambridge University Press, 1985).

4. UNCLH, TC, The Nottingham Connection, January 23 1987 (Mrs C. Mead).

5. Ibid. (Mrs W. Beuzeval).

6. See, for example, M. Wakelin, *English Dialects* (Athlone Press, 1972); M. Wakelin, *Patterns in the Folk Speech of the British Isles* (Athlone Press, 1972).

Chapter 4

THE STATE OF
THE ART

Today the student of oral testimony is better off than ever before when it comes to repositories with good quality tape holdings. The National Sound Archive of the British Library is the major national collection, but most regions now have one or more specialist units dealing with the general history of the area or some particular field of research. The North West Sound Archive at Clitheroe and the South Wales Miners' Archive at Cardiff are just two examples. However, the majority of tape collections have been welded on to existing institutions such as County Archives Offices, museums and libraries, and one of the problems faced by this branch of study over recent years has been the lack of a generally recognised place of deposit. Too often the preservation of oral data has owed more to the foresight and enthusiasm of particular individuals than to any clearly delineated policy — and, of course, in areas where such people have *not* taken the initiative the cause of oral history has tended to suffer.

In Nottinghamshire very little had been done before the emergence of two remarkable individuals, Robert Howard and Peter Wyncoll, in the early 1980s. Robert, a County Councillor, and Peter, a labour historian and official of the Trade Union NUPE, approached Nottingham University and the County Library Service to set up a joint project on the theme of 'Making Ends Meet: earning a living in Nottinghamshire, 1900-1950'. With the support of the Manpower Services Commission interviewers and secretaries were engaged and a two-year project resulted in the establishment of the Peter Wyncoll Archive in the Nottingham Central Library, Peter having tragically died in the early months of the project. Today the archive continues to function and provides a service for the people of the county, but its provision of new data was seriously impaired by the withdrawal of the MSC funding. Nevertheless, it at least provides a base for individuals and organisations who undertake recording work and who need a place of deposit for their findings. Over the long-term it is of paramount importance that all counties should have such a generally recognised central repository for research findings because without it a good deal of important material will certainly be lost.

Because of financial strictures which generally prevent the employment of a large number of paid researchers, oral archives of all sorts are heavily dependant on the voluntary work of individuals and organisations. And much good work is going forward. Alison McMorland took up residence with the Anglo-Scottish border shepherd Willie Scott to write *Herd Laddie o' the Glen*, a collection of the folk songs he knew and sang. Similarly, many adult education groups and local history societies have come to understand the importance of collecting information about specific communities. Indeed, this often proves to be an ideal starting point for a new research group. From a methodological point of view it gives new students the advantage of working back from the present to the past, and of progressing from familiar and easily assimilated ideas to more remote and complex ones. Moreover, it gets the local historian out into the community, meeting people, forging links, and making

Judy Kingscott, Assistant Librarian at the Nottinghamshire Local Studies Library, comparing a tape and transcript in the Peter Wyncoll Oral History Archive.

the inevitable discoveries. Most people would also recognise that it has the importance of 'rescue archaeology' because if it is not done quickly, very often the opportunity is lost for ever. So, as a starting point for a new society or adult class, the collection of oral data can be an important — and rewarding — challenge. However, although the data thus collected obviously remains the property of the society or group, it is desirable that either the original tapes and transcripts, or copies, should be deposited with the relevant county, or regional, co-ordinating agency, if it exists. Since locally kept records can so easily be misplaced or destroyed, someone within the group should be given the clear responsibility of transmission of data under some financial agreement which is acceptable to both the research group and the institution storing its material.

This sort of arrangement has been pioneered in Nottinghamshire, in a modest way, by the workings of the University Adult Education Department's Advanced Certificate in Local History. In the second year of that course there is a requirement that students should undertake two research workshops and one of these is traditionally earmarked as a study of oral testimony. In the context of this the group chooses a theme, and each student is made responsible for finding a respondent, interviewing that person, and then conducting the subsequent transcription and back-up work. In recent years the themes selected have been 'The civilian population in World War II', 'The development of entertainment and leisure' and 'National Service' — all of them within the context of Nottinghamshire. When all of the interview data is collected, the group is encouraged to compare notes and work out how it is collectively wiser about the theme under investigation. Finally, the tapes and transcripts are sent to the Oral History Archive of Nottingham Central Library to be copied and entered into the collection there. In this way one group of students can guarantee a regular supply of about fifteen tapes, an arrangement which is to everyone's benefit and might be usefully emulated elsewhere. In an age when too few resources are expended on history by central and county administrators it is an obvious expedient to keep the pot on the boil.

If adult researchers and students have an important role to play in the collection of oral testimony, the contribution that this area of study can make in the classroom is rather different. Although oral history projects have been attempted in schools, young people rarely have the maturity and perception to make really good interviewers. However, if it is presented properly to them, oral testimony can have a tremendous impact on their enjoyment and understanding of the past. To be successfully utilised in schools oral testimony needs to be presented in such a way as to make it accessible and digestible, and for this reason specially prepared 'study packs' are often the best way to proceed. In these, respondents are chosen as much for their communication skills as for the content of their interviews; interviews are to be conducted to fit into specific time slots or edited down; and associated photographs and documents are produced to underline the point that the interview is only a part of the totality of historical experience under examination. With thought and planning from experienced educationalists oral testimony can help raise the classroom experience of history above the levels of tedium which still sadly prevail in some schools. Moreover, the libraries and museums which hold the oral collections can make useful profits from the provision of such resources, profits which might be ploughed back into oral history in the form of equipment or salaries.

When we come to consider the use of edited extracts, rather than full-length interviews, many additional functions of oral testimony quickly spring to mind. One such use is in museums, where descriptive dialogue at 'listening points' might usefully be used to explain industrial or craft processes, or just to create 'atmosphere'. Another use might be in historical novels — which owe something to oral research, but which in essence are often highly romanticised. Popular recordings of dialect and anecdote are yet another means by which a flavour of the past might be brought before a wider public not generally involved with the study of 'history' in the true sense of the word.[1] This use and abuse of the past is perhaps best illustrated in the relationship between oral testimony and local radio. Radio producers by the very nature of their work deal with the spoken word as a stock-in-trade but often in a form in which it is reduced to its bare essentials. Like the newspaper editor, the radio journalist must often go for the quotation which says the most in the shortest time. Local radio producers have sometimes carried this attitude with them to their handling of oral testimony. Some have come to recognise it as a useful means of filling out time schedules which appeals to a predominantly elderly audience and fosters some feeling of local pride and identity. Many of the BBC local radio 'phone-ins' which flourished during the mid-1980s developed broadly historical themes, but failed to approach them with sufficient seriousness to do much good for the cause of oral history. All too often discursive 'nostalgia' was the order of the day.

However, some producers were more enlightened than that and, either by making their own feature or documentary programmes, or adapting the phone-in approach, they assisted ongoing projects or broke fresh ground for themselves. Mike Hapgood, Education Producer at BBC Radio Nottingham, helped initiate a number of important developments during the era of the Nottinghamshire project, once again underlining the extent to which co-operation between institutions can be very fruitful. The local radio station was able to assist in the search for respondents, to arrange programmes on themes of specific interest to the project, and initiate two major investigations on 'The Nottingham Underworld' and 'Local Industries'.[2] The last of these was arranged as a competition, with prizes for the best interviewees or authors of relevant written accounts. Once more, all parties stood to gain something. The project obtained respondents and information; the radio station produced programmes of good educational content; and the people of Nottinghamshire enjoyed the experience and had their awareness of the past brought into focus. Indeed, their concept of what history *was* may well have changed. Brought up on a diet of kings and queens during their own school days — with a dash of Robin Hood to spice the cake — many may have found it hard to believe that they themselves were now regarded as a relevant part of an historical process.

If in this instance the 'therapeutic' element of oral history was incidental, sometimes it is quite deliberate and goes far beyond the glimmers of understanding kindled by the Nottingham broadcasts. At the end of the day most 'academic' researchers are generally being quite selfish in that they are collecting for their own benefit, and that of future generations, rather than that of the respondents themselves — their welfare and sensitivities are important, of course, but they tend to be a secondary consideration. Not so in the approach of the Firebird Trust. The Trust is a voluntary body which 'aims to benefit the community and especially disadvantaged groups, through expressive and creative power of music and allied art forms'. In 1987 a project was organised at Bridlington under Stuart Bruce and Alison McMorland, in which a series of Edwardian concert evenings was organised for elderly people. After the concerts impressions and oral memories were put on tape in a series of fairly unstructured and impromtu interviews. When a wide range of material had been gathered it was edited and converted into blank verse for publication and an artist was engaged to produce drawings in keeping with the general tone of the reminiscences. The result was *Memories of the Edwardian Era* and a brief extract from the

section based on the recollections of Mrs Edith Wood will
suffice to illustrate the approach:

> My mother were always singing.
> She used always to start when she were cleaning,
> she was a good singer.
> She sang on the stage
> travelled all over.
> She married a showman, and
> I remember as a little girl
> travelling with the fairs.
> They 'ad these 'ere fairground organs y'know.
> As a child I used to man the dobby horses,
> it were a penny a ride.
> We travelled all over England.
> I were doing this for years till I got married
> then I left.
> I liked the life,
> it were better than settling down.
> When I see a caravan now
> I'm wanting to be with them.
> I think it gets in your bones.[3]

The end product is attractive both as a piece of poetry
and a visual experience, and no doubt the elderly people
who contributed to it benefited greatly from the exercise
and were justifiably proud to see their names in print.
However, purist oral historians would be critical of the
exercise because of the general vagueness of the chronology, the excess of editorial interference, and the fact that
the topics were only regarded as a means of producing
written copy and were seen as of little importance in their
own right. Within its own terms of reference *Memories of
the Edwardian Era* was a resounding success; according to
a more 'academic' standard of interpretation it might not
be regarded in that light.

An imaginative drawing by Michael Shepherd from the Firebird Trust publication *Memories of the Edwardian Era*. It relates to Tom Walker's memories of the Sick and Divide Club of Beeford and the important role, both practical and social, it played in the community. Reproduced by permission of the Firebird Trust.

The point proved by all this, of course, is that 'oral history' means different things to different people, and there are many quite justifiable ways of using spoken evidence about the past. This booklet has tended to lay emphasis on the 'academic' collection of oral data, perhaps the aspect most relevant to a research group or local history society, but museums, radio stations and voluntary bodies may well approach the task differently and, within their own terms of reference, achieve considerable success. Diversity leads to a richness of experience and interpretation, and most historians would only begin to draw a line when it appears that the past is becoming misinterpreted and exploited due to the overbearing imposition of contemporary requirements. This problem has already been encountered in the form of some politically motivated writers over the last twenty years, and most recently, perhaps, it is appearing in the commercially orientated eccentricities of some elements of the 'Heritage' business; talking dummies that recount tales of a bogus past do the cause of history little good. Oral testimony is now recognised as a source which can stand alongside more traditional written accounts and complement them in a unique fashion. It remains the obligation of all historians, both professional and amateur, to ensure that the memories of our forebears are not trivialised and are treated with the respect and seriousness which they deserve.

References

1. An example of a novel with a strong element of oral testimony is J. Wallace, *Independent Street* (Gowan, 1984); the record approach is represented by R. Scollins and J. Titford, *Ey Up Mi Duck! A Celebration of Derbyshire* (Stereo, Ram 1).

2. UNCLH, TC, The Nottingham Connection, Feb. 23, Mar. 22, May 10, June 14 1984, Dec. 12 1986, Jan. 16, Jan. 23, Jan. 30 1987.

3. S. Bruce and A. McMorland (eds.), *Memories of the Edwardian Era* (Firebird Trust, 1988), p. 10.